A BASIC BOOK OF
CANARIES
LOOK-AND-LEARN
by
LINDA A. LINDNER

The following is a list of photographers whose work appears in this book: Horst Bielfeld, Michael Gilroy, Harry V. Lacey, Ron & Val Moat, Horst Mueller (Vogelpark Walsrode), Michael DeFreitas, Kosmos Verlag, Mervin F. Roberts, P. Demko, Dr. Matthew M. Vriends, and Robert Pearcy. Illustrations by John Quinn.

Cover photograph of Yellow Border Fancy.

Distributed in the UNITED STATES to the Pet Trade by T.F.H. Publications, Inc., One T.F.H. Plaza, Neptune City, NJ 07753; distributed in the UNITED STATES to the Bookstore and Library Trade by National Book Network, Inc. 4720 Boston Way, Lanham MD 20706; in CANADA to the Pet Trade by H & L Pet Supplies Inc., 27 Kingston Crescent, Kitchener, Ontario N2B 2T6; Rolf C. Hagen Ltd., 3225 Sartelon Street, Montreal 382 Quebec; in CANADA to the Book Trade by Macmillan of Canada (A Division of Canada Publishing Corporation), 164 Commander Boulevard, Agincourt, Ontario M1S 3C7; in the United Kingdom by T.F.H. Publications, PO Box 15, Waterlooville PO7 6BQ; in AUSTRALIA AND THE SOUTH PACIFIC by T.F.H. (Australia), Pty. Ltd., Box 149, Brookvale 2100 N.S.W., Australia; in NEW ZEALAND by Brooklands Aquarium Ltd. 5 McGiven Drive, New Plymouth, RD1 New Zealand; in Japan by T.F.H. Publications, Japan—Jiro Tsuda, 10-12-3 Ohjidai, Sakura, Chiba 285, Japan; in SOUTH AFRICA by Multipet Pty. Ltd., P.O. Box 35347, Northway, 4065, South Africa. Published by T.F.H. Publications, Inc.

Manufactured in the United States of America by T.F.H. Publications, Inc.

SUGGESTED READING

  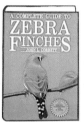 

T.F.H. offers the most comprehensive selections of books dealing with pet birds. A selection of significant titles is presented here; they and the thousands of other animal books published by T.F.H. are available at the same place you bought this one, or write to us for a free catalog.

  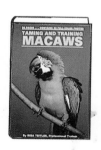

SUGGESTED READING

HANDBOOK OF MACAWS

DR. A.E. DECOTEAU

THE WORLD OF MACAWS

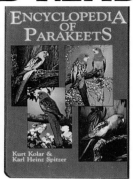

ENCYCLOPEDIA OF PARAKEETS

Kurt Kolar & Karl Heinz Spitzer

CONTAINS 30 FULL-COLOR PHOTOS AND DRAWINGS

PARROTS

By Dr. Matthew M. Vriends and Dr. Herbert E. Axelrod

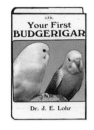

Your First BUDGERIGAR

Dr. J. E. Lohr

Budgerigars

Budgerigar Handbook

COMPLETE AND PRACTICAL BUDGERIGAR ENCYCLOPEDIA PROFUSELY ILLUSTRATED IN BOTH BLACK AND WHITE AND GLOWING COLOR

Parrots And Related Birds

Henry J. Bates and Robert L. Busenbark

BUDGIES AS PETS

The Proper Care of BUDGIES

CAGES AND AVIARIES

CURT AF ENEHJELM

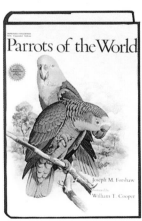

Parrots of the World

Joseph M. Forshaw

William T. Cooper

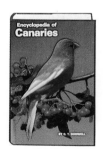

Encyclopedia of Canaries

BY G. T. DODWELL

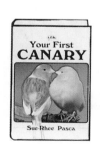

Your First CANARY

Sue-Rhee Pasca

CANARIES AS A NEW PET

Maja Müller Bierl

Cockatiels

16 Pages of Full-Color Photos Inside

COCKATIELS

BY NANCY CURTIS

CONTAINS 120 FULL-COLOR PHOTOS AND DRAWINGS

COCKATIELS

By Laura Tarlet

INTRODUCTION

Birds have enchanted individuals for centuries and are regarded as one of the most delightful creatures of nature. The canary is no exception to this rule. This little bird easily wins hearts with its beautiful plumage color, graceful motions, overall charm, and of course, the enjoyable sound of music from the male. As a pet in your home, the canary offers wonderful companionship. A sense of responsibility is implemented in young children as they share in the care. The existence of a canary in the home creates interest, passes time, and brightens each day. Canaries have an average life span of 8 to 10 years. The many varieties of canaries show the diversified way it is able to please its owner.

▶ A Self Green Canary. In domesticated birds the Self Green is the variety that most resembles the coloration of the wild canary.

◀ When we consider the current rich variety of colors, we see that the canary we know today has come a long way from its ancestor in the wild.

▶ As a result of selection and cross breeding, many breeds of domestic canaries no longer resemble the color or shape of the wild canary from which they originated.

INTRODUCTION

The canary has been bred in captivity for centuries. Many enthusiasts have taken to this hobby for the love of the species and are constantly trying to improve upon color, shape, and song.

◆ Canary breeding has become popular and specified. Countless varieties of colors and shades have come into existence through cross breeding. Canaries' colors are derived from pigmentation. There are three basic pigments: yellow, black and brown.

◆ Yellow Variegated Border Fancy. All type canaries were produced from selective breeding of mutations arising within broods of normal canaries.

◆ A canary is a hardy little bird that requires little maintenance from the owner. Proper care and a sound diet are reflected in your pet's overall appearance. A well kept bird will provide a lifetime of happiness for both the bird and owner!

HISTORY

The canary we are familiar with today originates from the Canary Islands, off the coast of Morocco. History tells us of 15th century sailors who trapped a small, melodious, grayish-green bird to take back to their homes in Spain. Soon after introduction, they quickly became popular pets and were traded to Germany, England, and eventually the world. Spain originally shipped only male canaries out to ensure its monopoly of the trade.

▲ The 19th century changed the Harz Mountain region of Germany into a mining center and canaries were used by miners to detect the presence of gas while digging. If the canary stopped singing or died, the mine workers were given advance warning of danger and would leave the mine.

▶ Two spectacularly well-colored Red-factor Canaries. Development of this bird has taken place over the last half-century.

▲ A Frilled Canary. Quite a lot has happened to the wild canary since it was first discovered. The posture canaries, for example, are much larger and definitely hold a different shape than the original wild canary. The Parisian Frill is currently the largest canary breed of all. Frilled Canaries are found in all color varieties including Red-factor. Color has little significance, however, when the birds are judged.

◀ A Lizard Canary, the oldest of all canary breeds. The markings on the feathers remind one of the scales on a lizard. They have become very popular as house birds because they are lively and present a very striking picture.

Italians did acquire females, and breeding to refine and improve the bird began. Canary breeding in Italy spread to Germany where bird and canary clubs were established toward the end of the 18th century. The Germans found the canary very valuable and became true masters in the development of the breed. The colors of canaries are rich in variety with shades varying greatly from the grayish-green we once knew. Canaries have been bred strictly for their color, shape, and song with new variations developing constantly.

◄ Canaries should have perches of a size that allow the claws on the longest toes to come into contact with the wood. Should your canary's nails need trimming, it is advised to take it to a reputable dealer or veterinarian so that the procedure may be demonstrated to you correctly.

◄ The fiery red colored variety of the canary owes its color to cross breeding the wild canary with a Red Hooded Siskin.

◄ The canary's crest is a mutation that occurred quite early. It has been known for at least 200 years. For a long time it was treated as a variation and not as a breed in its own right.

► A Border Fancy. The Border Fancy is a bird of curves and from any position one should be able to see smooth curves flowing into each other.

STOCK SELECTION

Specific considerations are involved in choosing a canary as a pet depending upon what is desired from the bird. Two important factors are song type and color. Prospective owners interested in a bird for song should be informed that only male canaries sing. Females will only give an occasional chirp. Today canaries come in such a variety of colors making it easy for one to be more desirable than another.

← When selecting your canary, keep in mind the traits you will most desire from your pet. To ensure an enjoyable experience with your new pet, be sure to purchase one that appears hardy and sound.

← It is best to view a variety of birds to assure that a good comparison has been made. Choosing a canary for color depends solely upon what appeals to the eye of the individual making the purchase.

◄ Distinguishing a male from a female is not an easy task. Years of experience are required to understand exactly what to look for in sexing young birds. Birds that are not in breeding condition are difficult to sex.

STOCK SELECTION

Choosing birds for breeding stock entails other considerations. A breeder may prefer a specific shape, color, or song variation, and will choose birds that best suit his needs. Overall, the number one priority to any decision is health. A healthy bird will appear active and have tight feathering and a substantial body weight.

◆ A White Gloster Fancy whose crest radiates well. A reliable pet dealer will give you a written guarantee stating that the bird being purchased is a male and that he will sing within an allotted period of time.

◆ The ideal age to buy a pet canary is between 6 and 9 months old. A breeding hen is best when under 3 years while a male may breed well into his 6th or 7th year.

◆ A natural perch can be offered to your canary providing it has not been chemically treated. Wood perches should be of different diameters to ensure proper exercise for the feet of the bird as well as to keep the nails trim. They should also be cleaned at least once a week.

◆ Color feeding is widely practiced among breeders. It is critical to begin color feeding a bird before it begins to molt so that the new feathers that are to grow will contain the coloring agent.

GENERAL CARE

Variations do exist in regard to the care of a canary. However, the basic principle is the same throughout. A routine will develop soon after the bird is home and both, bird and owner, have become accustomed. On the floor of the tray, place plain paper that is sized to line the bottom. Newspaper, a brown paper bag, or a paper towel are all suitable and prove to be inexpensive. On top of the paper, place a small handful of loose gravel. The canary eats the gravel to aid in digestion. The bottom of the cage can be cleaned as often as felt necessary with a minimum of at least once week. Two relatively large, shallow feeding cups of seed and one of water provide a sufficient daily food portion.

◀ A canary will spend most of its life inside a cage; therefore, sufficient room is required for it to exercise within.

➤ In addition to the regular diet, a moderate portion of dark, leafy greens and fresh fruits and vegetables may be offered, providing pesticides or insecticides have not been used.

➤ A variety of seeds should be offered to your canary on a daily basis.

➤ Frequent baths help to keep the canary's plumage in healthy condition. A canary will do best if kept in a peaceful spot, as cool as possible, but not in a draft. Keeping it too warm will cause a molt which brings the bird out of breeding condition and inhibits singing.

HAGEN

CANARY VEGETABLE FOOD

ART.#B-81 NET WT.170g(6OZ.)

➤ A canary is a bird with a high metabolism and requires a large amount of food. Canaries will eat whenever they are hungry, so, food should be available at all times.

◀ Perfectly adequate canary mixes are available at your local pet store or private breeder.

◆ Bright, colorful, and movable toys have a high appeal to most cage birds.

It is not advisable to allow a canary to fly outside of the cage. It is a relatively nervous bird that can cause injury to itself by flying into a mirror or window. Even worse, it may escape through an open door or window! ◀

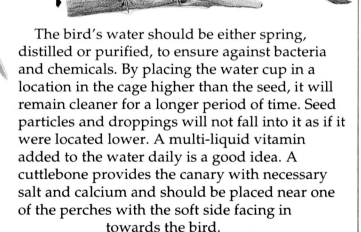

The bird's water should be either spring, distilled or purified, to ensure against bacteria and chemicals. By placing the water cup in a location in the cage higher than the seed, it will remain cleaner for a longer period of time. Seed particles and droppings will not fall into it as if it were located lower. A multi-liquid vitamin added to the water daily is a good idea. A cuttlebone provides the canary with necessary salt and calcium and should be placed near one of the perches with the soft side facing in towards the bird.

◆ Canaries are inquisitive creatures. Given the opportunity, they will investigate everything.

◆ Canaries enjoy bathing in cool water. A shallow dish may be placed on the floor of the cage or an outside bath that attaches to the door may be used.

ACCOMMODATIONS

Canaries are one of the few birds that are not destructive to their housing and can therefore be kept in all types of avicultural cages. The cages currently on the market are available in a variety of styles and colors and can easily be found to match all types of decor. They are often finished with chrome or brass plating which makes disinfecting the cage an easy task. Several doors in the cage make it easy to access the perches for cleaning. Seed and water cups are also made easily accessible from the outside. When selecting the cage, it is important to remember that the size must be sufficient to accommodate the needs of the canary. Toys, bird baths and hanging treats are all very well appropriate in the cage, but take up space and should be a prime consideration prior to purchasing. Providing the canary with ample room will keep it in good, healthy condition.

Plastic or Plexiglas bottoms help to avoid rust, which is a terrific hiding place for bacteria. The trays can be easily removed from the rest of the cage by either undoing a few clamps, or by sliding out.

Melanins are the most widespread pigments in the bird world and range in color from sand yellow to jet black.

ACCOMMODATIONS

A canary is not a bird to be handled on a regular basis and requires plenty of room in the cage to exercise. Square or rectangular shaped cages provide the most room for the bird. Height is of no importance, because birds fly back and forth, not upward and downward! ▶

◀ Variegated birds exhibit variable amounts of dark feathers. They are a mutation of the wild canary, which is a bird with pronounced melanin markings that are particularly apparent on the head, back, and wings.

The ideal cage offers the occupant plenty of room for free movement. Square or rectangular shaped cages provide the most flying room for your bird. ▶

◀ Canaries relate well to each other, but a single bird will sing more for you. If two male canaries are housed together, they will fight during breeding season and a male housed with a female will not sing.

ACCOMMODATIONS

The outdoor aviary is a popular form of housing among bird keepers. On the average, an aviary is the size of a chicken coop, and can house any number of birds. Canaries do very well in aviaries, and with proper protection, may stay outdoors all year. To ensure the well being of the birds an aviary requires major considerations such as proper construction, location, and maintenance. The floor base can be either of dirt or concrete, the latter being the more sanitary and rodent resistant. Treated wood for the individual dividing frames is best, and as a further preservative, creosote can be used.

A suitable size wire mesh will keep the birds in, as well as unwanted guests out. A sturdy mesh will prove better to the life of the aviary. Galvanized welded wire with a hole dimension of ½ in x 1in is normally used.

➡ An aviary that has wire mesh attached to each side of the frame will have a 2 in. gap between each mesh layer keeping all clawed animals a safe distance away from the birds.

➡ An aviary is an ideal housing facility providing it is used in a wise manner. Aviaries can house a great number of birds, however, all birds that are to be housed together should be compatible.

J.R. QUINN

◗ The Red-Factor Canary makes for a colorful and attractive pet. Red factors housed in an aviary require natural color enhancers but artificial color agents will turn all of the birds in the aviary red.

ACCOMMODATIONS

The front side of the aviary must face the south as much as possible so that the birds can be protected from cold winds and driving rain. During winter months, a covering of heavy plastic attached to the frame will add protection.

Your aviary can add to the beauty of your yard. In most canary breeds, the plumage is a mixture of dark and light colors. The many different color varieties will enhance its appearance even more. ▶

◀ Large, walk-in outdoor aviaries are practical for housing a large number of birds. The floor of an aviary should have a slight slope incorporated away from the shelter to take the rainwater away.

◀ Even those considered to be aggressive often get on very well together in an aviary; however, territorial disputes may occur during breeding season. It is advisable to keep an eye on such birds to ensure the safety of all occupants.

◀ Location of an outdoor aviary is important. It should be sited where it will be partially shaded and not exposed to extremely windy conditions.

SINGING CANARIES

A singing canary adds enthusiasm to a home and is very good company. A dark, dreary house seems to come alive when a canary begins to sing. A recorded tape of singing birds will entice your bird to become more vocal. ◗

Canaries purchased in pet stores are admired mostly for their ability to sing. A pet store will keep its stock of singing birds in single, box-like cages because canaries tend to sing more when separated from other birds. This is the best way to view and purchase a singing canary. Male canaries sing to attract females.

The female canary does not sing. A male paired with a female will only sing when it is ready to mate. Two male canaries should not be kept in the same cage together if they are to be song birds, because they will spend much of their time together fighting.

◖ All varieties of male canaries are able to sing. However the songs will vary. The best way to select a canary for song is entirely according to your own taste, as far as internal appearance and song are concerned.

It is, however, beneficial to have two canaries in the same house. Keep them separate but visible to each other. This creates competition between the two, because they are able to hear and see one another but not come in contact with each other. Chances are the amount of song will increase.

◖ A Frosted Red-Factor Canary. Not only does the coloring of this bird light up a room, its song can enchant the hearts of all those it encounters.

SINGING CANARIES

Proper conditions, correct diet and plenty of exercise, will maintain healthy and happy birds that will continue to sing for a long time.

▶ Birds of unusual colors (orange, red, white, and slate gray) sometimes have loud and shrilly sounding songs because they have been bred for color and not for song.

▶ Male canaries will sing more often when kept singly. If a bird's housing is the right size and it receives a proper diet, it will be happy and will sing more.

It is likely that while trying to select a bird, you will be able to see it sing. This means that relatively little time is spent by the buyer trying to hear the birds sing, and a choice is easier to make. A person who is looking for a particularly good songster needs some time to listen to the songs of different birds, and then a choice depends entirely according to one's own taste. ▶

◀ There is an astonishing number of color varieties among canaries available in pet shops today. Many different color varieties will appeal to you because of their uniqueness. One must keep in mind that the health of the bird is more important than its beauty.

SONG VARIETIES

Two of the oldest and best known breeds of song canaries are the Harz Roller and the Waterschlager. The Harz Roller originated in Germany and has been bred exclusively for the quality of its song for over 200 years. The Roller, as we have come to know it, set the standard for all other singing canaries. The name is derived from the rolling way in which the bird delivers its song. It is soft and melodious and is always produced with a closed bill. Neither type nor color is of importance when it comes to good singing. It is important that the Waterschlager and the Harz Roller are not crossed with each other. This does not improve their songs, but it detracts from the beauty of each.

◗ It is believed that various machines and assorted contraptions were made to produce sounds that were like water flowing over rocks which the Roller learned to imitate. Today, a breeder will retain his best singing stock to act as tutors for the offspring produced that year.

◖ Good song is not hereditary, it must be learned. Young males learn to sing from imitating older birds. Records and tapes of singing birds also serve as learning devices for young birds.

The song of the Waterschlager is more varied than that of the Roller. It is a wilder type of song, more natural and impassioned. ◗

SONG VARIETIES

The Waterschlager originated in Belgium by breeders who wanted to produce a variety of song all their own. Their voice is versatile, and their song is more varied than the Roller. The Waterschlager is a slightly larger, stockier bird, bred exclusively in a pure yellow color. Another variety that should be mentioned, due to its quickly gaining popularity, is the American Singer. Cultivated in the United States, its song resembles that of the Harz Roller. Other valued characteristics include color, soft plumage, and a good carriage. It is still considered a new variety and in the early stages of its development.

← Neither type nor color is of importance in a good Roller Canary. The song of a canary is constantly trying to be improved upon. The song of a canary should not be too loud or too shrillish.

← The Brown Border Fancy is of wild-type coloration. It has little visual appeal to most pet bird keepers but has excellent singing capabilities.

The Roller Canary, world famous for the beauty of its song, took several centuries for breeders in Germany to produce such a bird. ▶

FROSTED

An intensive bird has the same amount of coloring as a non-intensive, but shorter feathers. Frosting occurs in all color variations and is preferred by breeders to be even throughout the entire body. ◀

▶ A Frosted Yellow Canary. The actual shade of coloring can vary considerably and is controlled by sex, heredity, and feeding.

A non-intensive bird has more room for the same amount of coloring because of its larger feathers. The intensity of the color is somewhat diminished by the white edges. ▶

Frosting in a canary refers to the absence of color at the ends of the feathers. Once an undesirable trait in coloring, frosting is now accepted by breeders providing it is equal throughout the entire body. The best example of what makes a canary frosted is the common yellow canary. A good yellow canary should be strong in color over its entire body, but variations in the depth of coloring are common and clearly visible. The breast, rump, and crown tend to be a noticeably deeper, more intense shade than the wings and tail.

Looking closely, it is obvious that the most intensely colored parts are made up of short feathers. In other words, a short feather has the same amount of coloring distributed in it as a long feather. A long feather is therefore referred to as less intensively colored because it must make do with the same amount of coloring as a short one.

◄ Variations in the depth of coloring are common and clearly visible. Most people who purchase a canary to be a pet in the home are not concerned with the bird's color, but more interested in its singing ability.

◄ Canaries are bred to emphasize certain characteristics, often at the expense of the breeds. A canary that is bred for song will not have the excellence of form that is normally found in the breed.

The intensity of the color of this Frosted Canary is somewhat diminished by the white edges. Providing toys for your bird help to keep it active and prevent boredom. ◄

◄ A non-intensive bird is referred to as "frosted" because he has almost no color in the tips of his feathers, and the outer hooklets possess no color at all giving the bird a whitish top layer appearance.

VARIEGATED

Variegation is the term used to refer to the loss of melanin in some areas, in turn, due to a mutation. It occurs in all living species. Melanin is a pigment that naturally occurs within the body and does not depend on food intake. It is the most widespread pigment in the bird world and ranges from sand yellow to jet black. Breeders refer to it as all dark colors.

← Variegation basically occurs in four areas; frontal, naped, saddled, and bridled. Variegated birds can have more light areas than dark, or be heavily variegated— more dark feathers than light.

← Variegation is not sex-linked, it is a stage between melanin birds and clear birds. A piebald appearnace is caused by the localized absence of melanin and is well known to us in regard to all domestic animals.

← Melanin synthesis is a complex process. What the dark colors look like is influenced by mutations concerning melanin density and type, and feather structure.

← A Yellow Variegated Border Fancy. Variegated birds have been bred for centuries. Breeders paired partially variegated birds with each other and obtained completely clear birds as well as very beautiful variegated canaries.

Variegated markings on a canary are usually symmetrical. Only symmetrically variegated birds can be considered for competition at shows. Variegation of show birds must occur in specific areas of the plumage. ☚

☚ This Silver-Gray Canary's plumage consists of melanin colored feathers throughout its body.

A Blue White Agate Canary. Agate birds are said to have been in existence more than 250 years ago. This well-established mutation has prominent facial markings, called "whiskers," which stand vertically under the eyes. ▸

Clear canaries are those without any presence of melanin, pure white, yellow, and red. Frontal variegation consists of dark patches on the forehead, chin or eyebrows. Variegation of the nape is when dark patches are present on the back of the neck and are able to extend as far as the eyes and the sides of the neck. In saddle variegated birds, only the upper feathers of the wings are variegated. Bridle variegated refers to the stripes which extend from the base of the bill to the eyes and occasionally beyond.

▸ The inheritance of Variegated birds is such that there are always pure, unvariegated birds among the offspring.

BORDER FANCY

The Border Fancy was developed by breeders who wished for a smaller type canary than the Norwich, Yorkshire, and Lancashire breeds that predominated the time. Through cross breeding with Harz Rollers, small Norwich and Lizard canaries, the Border Fancy breed was perfected.

The Border Fancy has become one of the most popular breeds of canaries. Well loved for its singing ability, the Border Fancy comes in many varieties of color. ▶

Many of the color varieties of canaries available today still consist of yellow and green like their ancestors. The Border Fancy has become one of the most popular type canaries in many countries so far. ▶

A very important advantage of the Border Fancy is its reliability and its eagerness to breed. The Border Fancy is a neat, dainty and confiding bird. It is highly recommended to the novice breeder. ▶

At the time it was perfected, it was one of the smallest breeds, but styles changed and the birds were being bred for more of a larger head. This made them similar to the Norwich and it soon became a fault. Once again, the breed required perfecting.

BORDER FANCY

It did not take long for its popularity to be regained as a rounded, yet elegant bird. It is a highly recommended bird to the novice breeder because it does not have any of the characteristics or postures that are so difficult to obtain in most other breeds, and it is prolific. The Border Fancy was originally only 13 cm in length and was known as the "Wee Gem" because of its size. Through the years its size has increased to 15 cm which has become the standard.

▲ The Border Fancy is known for its alertness. Careful selection of well colored stock is essential. Its soft, silky plumage comes in all colors except red.

▲ The Border Fancy is a great delight to everyone who appreciates simple, natural beauty. Its body is well rounded yet elegant and it is capable of singing a variety of songs.

▶ The Border Fancy's feathers lie close to its body and are firm with a fine, smooth appearance. The Border Fancy should not have long, rough feathering.

◀ A Border Fancy Hen. The good roundness of the breast shows the good breeding capability and hatching potential of this bird.

FRILLED

Frilled Canary varieties are desired by breeders of style. The posture of all frilled varieties is unique from other posture breeds. The bird firmly straightens itself out by raising its shoulders and extending its neck well forward. At the same time its head is pulled down, making the head and neck come forward in a horizontal line.

← A Yellow Variegated Frilled Canary displaying the principal kinds of frills from long, flowing fine feathers to short, crisper ones with tight curling.

The Frilled Canaries are named for the way in which the back, chest and thighs carry curled feathers. The popularity of the Frilled Canary is increasing everywhere in the world. It is one of the most favored breeds at shows and always receives the most recognition. ▶

The Belgian Frill is believed to be the result of cross breeding between the Parisian Frill and the Belgian Canary. This grotesque, long-legged, odd and unnaturally hunched bird is very unusual looking but graceful and delicate in movement. Frills are not bred for any specific color. All colors exist.

Several frilled varieties exist and differ in how and where their feathers are frilling. The most prominent varieties are, Parisian, Northern Dutch, and Belgian Frill. With the Frilled Varieties, much inbreeding is necessary to maintain the characteristics of the breed. Because the birds are closely related, one sometimes gets individuals that are blind in one eye or both.

The Frilled Canary's plumage is long and soft with a fine structure.

The Northern Dutch Frill is second largest in size among Frill canaries. This large, sturdy, upright breed originated in northern France. A Dutch Frilled Canary is slightly smaller and not as frilly or curly as a Parisian Frill.

The Frilled Canary appeals to interest in novelty. It is not a very hardy strain.

Special combs and brushes are often used by exhibitors to ensure the direction the feathers lie.

The Parisian Frill is currently the largest and most impressive breed of all. Originating in France, it has enjoyed popularity for over one hundred years. Curling or frilling of feathers occurs most extensively in the Parisian Frilled Canary.

GLOSTER FANCY

The charming little Gloster Fancy has become the most widely distributed of all form varieties. The feathers above the eyes of a Gloster Fancy should be well-developed. They should be so broad that one is unable to see the eyes when viewed from above. ▶

← Gloster Canaries are small birds, that are most commonly characterized by a crest consisting of a group of feathers radiating from a common center on top of the head.

← The Gloster Fancy came about through a cross breeding of the Norwich, (known for its long feathers that give a fluffy appearance), the Crested Canary, (which was only thought to have been a variation and never treated as its own breed), and the small Border.

The Gloster Fancy is typically characterized by a crest on its head called a corona. A Gloster with the crest absent is called a consort. The feathers of a consort surrounding the eyes are very well developed. When looking down upon the bird it is impossible to see its eyes because the eyebrow feathers are so broad. It is of critical importance to be aware that two corona birds can not be paired together for breeding. Because of a lethal gene, a corona must always be bred to a consort.

GLOSTER FANCY

The Gloster Fancy is available in all colors. This Yellow Variegated Corona is a most common color variety.

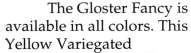

A Green Variegated Gloster Fancy. Gloster Fancies come in a variety of colors except red. This breed is not color fed nor has it ever been crossed to a siskin because it would lose its size.

The Gloster Fancy is becoming quite popular due to the uniqueness of its looks and its qualities as a good singing pet.

The Gloster Fancy is a small, round, compact bird that is lively and bold. Gloster Fancy's are prolific and eager to breed. They raise their young with no difficulties and both parents have a hand in rearing the young. The Gloster Fancy occurs in all colors except the Red-factor. Most commonly, they are seen in yellows, greens, browns, whites and variegated.

The Gloster is an ideal singing house pet as well as a show bird. Glosters also are such good parents that they are often used as foster parents for those birds that do not feed their young.

LIZARD

The distinctive coloration of the plumage best characterizes the Lizard as a color variety. The plumage is extremely thick and the feathers are slightly stronger in structure than those of color canaries. ▶

← The red color in this Lizard Canary is the result of both gene action and feeding. The Lizard is one of the few canaries not named after its place of origin, but rather for its markings.

The Lizard Canary is a very special breed. It is neither bred for shape nor color and it does not hold itself in any unusual posture. Every one of the outline feathers has a light, bleached looking margin which gives the appearance of scales as on a lizard, the basis for its name.

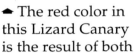

← The scaly pattern of the Lizard Canary is due to a mutation. The most common Lizard Canaries are those with a yellow ground color.

A Bronze Lizard Canary with a wide and well developed cap. In breeding, it is best to pair together birds that will produce young resulting in showing their scaling best. ▶

The Lizard's head is of lighter colored feathers and is simply called the "cap." The characteristic scales are called "spangles." The less, well-developed scales on the underside are known as "rowings." It is imperative that during the Lizard's molt it is watched very carefully for feather picking because not every feather will grow back with the same color and markings every time.

▲ A Lizard Canary, capped and with a series of black crescent shaped spots running in orderly parallel rows down the back of the bird.

◀ Everyone of the contour feathers of the Lizard Canary has a light, bleached-looking margin.

➥ This Clear-Capped Gold Lizard shows the breast markings well, but, little can be seen of the spangling on the back.

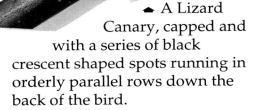

The bird will appear spotted rather than scaled when it picks its feathers during molting. The Lizard is a reliable breeder, with both the male and female caring for the young.

NORWICH

Early on, Norwich Canaries were developed to be a light, slim bird with a pure and particularly strong plumage being their chief characteristic. By crossing the small Norwich with the Lancashire, (the largest canary ever bred and now very rare,) large, long feathered birds were produced. The head structure of the Norwich is broad, strong and has almost no transition to the neck.

▲ The origin of the Norwich is not exactly known, however, the breed was perfected in England and it received its name from the city that was the breeding center, Norwich.

The heavily bodied Norwich is among one of the largest canary breeds. In the past, Norwich canaries were much lighter and slimmer ▼

▲ Breeders of the Norwich turned their attention from color to size. Larger birds with fuller plumage did result, however, the breed was ruined because their identity had been lost. It took strict breeding selection to return this breed to its special type.

The Norwich has a quiet and placid disposition and is actually quite undemonstrative. If housed alone, it is a good idea to add a lively bird such as, another variety of canary or a Peking Robin, in with the Norwich to teach it how to interact with other birds.

NORWICH

Many breeders strictly raise Norwich and are very successful with the outcome. Norwich Canaries are extremely devoted parents and rear their young very well. ➤

A Norwich Canary. The ideal bird of this breed is characterized primarily by its head, which is large and well rounded, with almost no transition from its neck to the rest of its body.

The feathers of the Norwich are long and of silky softness. They envelop the bird smoothly all over. In the 1800's the feathers began to create cysts under the skin because they were so soft that they could not penetrate through the skin. It was not until around 1950, that strict selection and cross breeding, 'revived' the breed to its special type and health. Its plumage was to be soft, long, and full, but not shaggy.

◄The solid, heavy figure of the Norwich attracts the attention of all show visitors. They make a nice cage bird, but require larger accomodations because of their size.

RED FACTOR

The red factor is now used as an under-color for pigment canaries. ◆

The wild canary has a natural yellow basic color. Cross breeding with the Red Hooded Siskin produced, what we now call, the Red-Factor canary. The red coloring of the siskin, as well as the yellow of the canary, is known as a lipochrome, a naturally occurring pigment that is soluble in fats and oils, also called a carotenoid. Cross breeding these two assured that the red was incorporated in the birds' hereditary material and therefore was able to transform suitable plant substances into the red lipochrome. Canaries intake carotenoids with food. Greens and carrots are particularly good sources.

A pigmented Red Canary. The red coloring of the canary is derived from carotenoid substances in the bird's diet. Natural carotene additives are available in a powder or liquid form and may be added to the food supply to enhance the natural red color of the bird. ◆

Breeders tried to develop a strain of red canaries for a number of years. It was discovered that the Red Hooded Siskin Finch would mate with a canary and produce fertile young.

RED FACTOR

In addition to inheriting the colors of the Red Hooded Siskin, Red-Factor Canaries also have the clear, liquid voice of their canary ancestors.

The Red-Factor is a relatively new breed that has rapidly become one of the most desired Canaries. The colors of the best birds are very deep red-orange, pink, apricot, red-bronze, and copper.

Because of the lovely song and striking appearance of these beautiful birds, they are usually more expensive than the other varieties. The Red-factor exists in a variety of shades ranging from a pale apricot to a deep firey red. The shade of a bird can be modified with a coloring agent added to the diet.

Their body transforms lipochromes, in the liver, into specific color molecules which act in accordance with the birds' genetic make-up. These color molecules are transported in the bloodstream to the quills of the feathers where they crystallize in the keratinizing feather tissue. This occurs only during molting season. Optimal feed containing carotene is essential, with the red color varieties, if the birds' are not given sufficient quantities of fresh plants at regular intervals.

YORKSHIRE

The Yorkshire is a large, elegant breed that developed in Yorkshire England in 1870. Originally, the goal of breeders was to develop a long, slender bird covered with soft silky feathers. The original Yorkshire did not have the broad shoulders that are so characteristic of it today. Soon after the turn of the century, breeders became interested in larger birds.

A Yorkshire Canary. This Blue Variegated White bird is a rare and hard to obtain variety. The Yorkshire's head is nicely rounded, with the back of it being quite prominent.

◀ The large and slender body build of the Yorkshire makes it stand out in a crowd. Yorkshires are trained for their posture by having greens laid on top of their cages with the perches inside at the appropriate height to require them to stretch. The silky textured plumage is short, tight and held close to the body.

The Yorkshire Canary is a particularly elegant and large breed of type canary. Color is of secondary importance in the Yorkshire, size is number one. The pureness and eveness of color are of importance when it comes to showing. All colors and variegations are permitted. ▸

YORKSHIRE

The Yorkshire's erect posture and its sturdy, yet slender, streamline shape make it an extraordinary sight to behold.

A Variegated Yorkshire Canary showing the desirable fullness in head, neck, and breast. ▶

The Yorkshire has become known as a posture type canary with a length of 17-19cm. Plumage is tight and smooth all over. Yorkshire Canaries are very reliable breeders and raise their young without problems. The male ususally takes a very active part in rearing the young. The breeding procedure is very strenuous for the hen, therefore, the pair should only be allowed 2 or 3 broods per season.

Due to the large size and weight of the bird, it is advisable to put a marble, slightly larger than the eggs, in the nest so that eggs are not crushed during incubation. A more spacious cage is also required for the Yorkshire to allow it the proper amount of exercise. The posture is erect and sturdy, yet slender, with long, extended legs that give it an even larger appearance.

◀ The color of a Yorkshire is of no importance. It is bred strictly for its size and posture.

SCOTCH FANCY

When the Scotch Fancy poses, its nicely arched head-back-tail line becomes very evident. With its legs held tightly flexed, the Scotch Fancy pulls its head forward and down while lifting its shoulders. Simultaneously, the tail is pressed towards the perch. The breast does not protrude but, curves inward. These birds do not stand in this exaggerated position without training and an inherited predisposition. Until the beginning of the 20th century, it was a very popular breed in Scotland and England. The numbers then dwindled and the bird almost became extinct. Not until quite recently did the breed begin to flourish again.

Because of their rarity and novel appearance, Scotch Fancies are very expensive.

The Scotch Fancy is seldom seen except at canary shows. Color is of no importance, but the Scotch Fancy must possess neat, tight fitting feathers, and a small head.

The Scotch Fancy originated in Scotland where the name 'bird o' circlë' was attributed because it stood in a half circle position.

The Scotch Fancy Canary adopts its odd stance only after much training.

The Scotch Fancy's posture is still being perfected by a few dedicated breeders.

COLOR IN THE CANARY

The wild canary is a natural yellow color with dark brown to blackish streaks. All color varieties that we are familiar with today originated from this bird through cross breeding and mutations. First, partially clear birds occurred, then variegated, and finally entirely clear birds, the first yellow canaries. Since then, countless colors and marking combinations have arose and new colors are always being introduced.

◄ All different color varieties of canaries have developed from the greenish-yellow wild canary.

▲ Variegation is determined by genes. It is the natural proportion of light and dark pigments on the body.

A Red-Factor Canary. There is a large variety of coloration in the Red-Factor series.

At present, the canary can be bred in more than 500 different color varieties. The range of canary colors achieved is wide and it takes many years of experience and accurate breeding records to achieve a desired color blend.

Variegation was among one of the first mutations resulting from selection and cross breeding the wild canary. ▶

◄ The White Canary is only a color variation of the existing canary types.

▲ The Border Fancy Canary does not have any of the characteristics or postures that are so difficult to breed for in other varieties.

HEALTH CARE

◀ A well fed, well housed, and clean kept bird poses little need for medicine and remedies, but, this does not mean that the bird will never fall ill, it is only a good preventative.

A hospital cage should be small so that the ill bird can remain calm and peaceful. Each time a sick bird recovers and is removed, the hospital cage requires disinfection. ◀

An ill canary does not sit properly on its perch, its feathers are fluffed out and its head droops. The bird shows little interest in anything, especially its food. Its eyes are not wide open nor bright. Droppings also change from normal to either loose or very hard. A bird in this condition should be moved and isolated to a smaller cage that will confine it and keep it as stable as possible.

◀ Branches and natural perches should be free of parasites and insecticides. If you are unsure of the safety of the branch, do not use it. You may choose to purchase one from a lumber yard to keep your mind at ease.

Fluffed feathers, when seen in an otherwise normally sleek-looking bird, should always be investigated. This condition could mean that illness is present.

This smaller cage is often referred to as a hospital cage and must be warmed to a temperature of 85-90° F. All food, other than seed and water, should be discontinued. Antibiotics and other medications can be administered in the drinking water. After the ill bird has recovered, it should be acclimated slowly back to a lower temperature. The hospital cage should be thoroughly disinfected to rid it of any pathogens.

◀ Frequent bathing will help keep your bird's feathers healthy. Drafts after bathing should be avoided because a serious illness can develop.

▲ Very often, by the time a person realizes a bird is sick, it is too late to help it. Awareness of the first signs of illness helps in guarding against unnecessary fatalities.

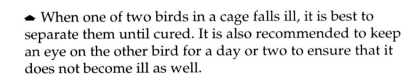

▲ When one of two birds in a cage falls ill, it is best to separate them until cured. It is also recommended to keep an eye on the other bird for a day or two to ensure that it does not become ill as well.

◀ Diarrhea can develop from overeating of watery greens such as lettuce or celery. Darker greens are more vitamin enriched and will not cause harm.

TAMING

A canary can gradually be trained to eat seeds from your hand. This can be accomplished by holding your hand in the cage, with seeds in the palm, for a few minutes each day until the canary becomes used to your hand.

Taming and training a canary is nearly impossible with more than one bird in a cage. It should be kept separately with no disturbances. It is important that all of the bird's attention is focused on you and not on other birds

A canary is a naturally nervous and flighty bird that should be kept away from all hasty movements.

Canaries have a natural fear of movement, especially overhead, and do not like to be handled. They do not display affection as other birds, and tend to be somewhat flighty. Although not advisable because of accidents that can occur, canaries can be let out of their cage to fly free, and trained to fly back on their own. Keeping canaries separately increases their training ability. If they are housed together they will not want to be bothered with people.

Two male canaries must never be kept in the same cage. Not only will the birds sing a lot less, they may also attack one another. It is advisable to keep a small light on at night time so that the bird can see in case it becomes frightened.

Everyday that a canary comes to know and trust you, it will become more tame.

➤ You may wish to allow your canary to fly around the house and train it to fly back to the cage on its own.

A bird that is allowed more exercise requires more food than does an untrained one. By using a treat as a reward, for a tame bird, you will inspire it to keep up a high standard.

After about two weeks in its new environment, the bird is reasonably familiar with the room it is in. It can then be let out of its cage. Do not chase the bird out, however, just open the door. Sooner or later the bird will notice the opening. Food should not be placed outside of the cage. When the bird is tired or hungry, it will find its way back into its cage, and then the door may be closed.

Train birds separately at first, then, train in pairs and trios so they will be company for each other.

➤ With patience, you can teach your canary to perch on your hand. To do so, remove the perch and position the cage so that it is at eye level. Insert a pencil or finger into the cage and try gently to induce the bird to perch.

BREEDING CONDITION

To condition the birds it is best to set them up in single cages, but, visible to each other. When canaries are ready to mate, they will begin calling to one another, and the male will begin to feed the female.

The Birds are in breeding condition when the male is in full song and the female's nest is built. She will begin to sit for most of the day. A female in breeding condition will lay eggs, even if she is not paired with a male

Canaries tend to become aggressive during breeding season. Keep a watchfull eye on these birds because they could harm or even kill one another.

Breeding begins in mid February. Matched pairs should be selected about six weeks prior to breeding so that they may come into the proper breeding condition. By this we mean a physical state in which the birds are ready to mate. A healthy male that is ready to mate will show a "spike" in the form of a projection of skin around the cloaca when the feathers of the abdomen are blown away. The belly will be slightly sunken and of a normal flesh color.

BREEDING CONDITION

Canaries intended for breeding are best purchased in the fall when the molt is over and the birds have all their new plumage.

The diet for breeding birds should be of as wide a variety as possible. Canaries will not feed anything new to their young and need to be accustomed to foods that will put weight on the chicks once hatched.

The male will also be in full song. The hen canary will have a slightly more elongated body. The cloacal region is not as prominent as in the cock bird. If a small "spike" is present, it points rather more towards the tail. The female should have a nest made available so that she may begin building when ready.

Larger varieties of canaries require larger breeding cages. For any type of bird, the larger the living space available, the better.

One male canary can be paired with two or three different females in a given year. Do not remove the male from one female before the chicks produced have fledged. Very often the male assists in feeding the young. A good male can produce as many as fifty young in a given season.

NEST SELECTION

◀ Plastic and wire mesh nests are easy to wash and disinfect each season and last a long time, proving to be economical. Wicker nests are not as sustainable and usually need to be thrown away after each season because disinfecting causes the structure to weaken. Some breeders even prefer to disinfect or change a bird's nest after each clutch of young to ensure against parasites. Instead of this, one may choose to dust the nest with flea powder.

A brood of recently fledged Yorkshires. Larger birds will require larger nesting sites as well as larger breeding cages in order to house the parents and all the chicks comfortably. ➡

Good nest building materials are fibers, wool, grass, hay, and coconut. Do not use cotton or any type of material that can fray and become entangled. Very often invisible fibers wrap around the legs of birds and cut off circulation.

Nesting material is provided during mating and the hen builds the nest herself. A male will try to help the female by picking up some nest material and bringing it to her for placement. ◆

NEST SELECTION

◆ The female canary builds the nest. She becomes an ambitious builder and sometimes will construct a nest with two openings, one for her tail and one for her head. It is advised to sew a few stiches in the felt of the nest so that the male does not rip it out and destroy the nest.

A wide range of different styles of nests are available for canaries. The most common variety are hemispherical shaped, offered in wicker, wire mesh, and plastic. All nests are constructed with holes in the bottom to provide ventilation to the clutch. Nests are equipped with handy fittings so that they can be attached to the walls or to the front of the cage. For nesting, firm material is best. From this, the hen will construct a very good nest. Nest liners of a coarse felt are a good idea and give the bird a basic shape to follow along with in building.

◆ Canaries can complete the construction of the nest in two or three days, once a suitable nesting site has been decided upon. The first egg will be laid shortly after this.

◆ A hen canary uses her bill and feet to give the nest its right size and shape by turning around in it a number of times.

PAIRING

Both the male and female should be of good breeding stock. Canaries are paired together according to color specifications of the breeder.

Toward mating time, the male will begin to sing to attract a female. This is why a male sings more during the cooler months. The breeding season begins in mid-February and lasts until late June. After this, it is advised to throw away any eggs the female might lay to inhibit her from raising another clutch. ▬

◆ The male and female should be separated from each other but kept visible. After 4 or 5 days, they may be placed together to feed each other and finish their courtship

◆Both the male and female are in good feathering because they have just completed their molt. At this time they are usually in the best of health and will come into breeding condition rather quickly.

There are certain color combinations that should not be paired together, such as white x white or crested x crested, because of a lethal gene. The main goal of the breeder is to produce offspring that are most in demand by the public and that will better the future of their own breeding stock.

▶ For the novice breeder, obtaining two healthy specimens requires the help of a good breeder or pet store owner. Both the male and female should have tight feathering that lies close to the body. They should not sit lathargically, but rather lively.

Breeding pairs should be properly matched. Certain color combinations can not be matched together such as white to white, or crested to crested. Pairing such birds together results in a reduced number of young, that die soon after hatching, or die within the egg. ▲

▲ A new breeder should decide on whether to breed for color or for song. Rarely does one breed a pair of birds expecting to accomplish both.

The mating pair should have good size for their variety and no defects. Physical defects, of course are of no concern, only those of the genetic origin. ▶

EGG HANDLING

At this time in the incubation process, the canary hen should be kept undisturbed so that she does not abandon her nest. ➤

A female canary will lay her first egg five to ten days after the first copulation. She will then lay one egg, every day, early in the morning. In the wild, birds do not begin to incubate their eggs as soon as they are laid. Incubation does not actually begin until after the fourth egg has been laid. By doing this, the clutch hatches on or about the same day. Domestic birds, however, begin incubation immediately after the first egg is laid. By doing so, the clutch hatches on successive days making the brood different sizes and virtually, the smallest hatchling dies.

➤ Dummy eggs are used in the nest until the female has laid her entire clutch. This ensures that the young will hatch on or about the same day.

A female that is of breeding age and in condition will lay eggs regardless of fertility. A canary will lay anywhere from four to six eggs. ▶

This makes it necessary to remove the eggs from the nest when they are laid, and replace them with artificial ones until the fourth egg is laid. At this time all of the original eggs may be replaced. From this point, the incubation lasts from 13 to 14 days and it is almost certain that all chicks will hatch on the same day.

◄ This pair of Lizard Canaries will be kept very busy. New born chicks eat tremendous amounts of food relative to their size.

◄ These chicks are only a few days old. In a couple more weeks they will be able to feed themselves and hop about.

Hemispherical shaped nests provide a good structure for the female canary to build her nest. When using any fine nesting material, be sure strands are short enough that the bird's feet cannot become entangled. ◄

WEANING THE YOUNG

The male canary will feed the female and she then passes the predigested food onto her young. When the young are several days old, the hen begins to leave the nest for short periods of time, and the male aids in feeding the young directly. ▸

For some hobbyists, nothing beats the satisfaction of raising a canary family. At times, some hobbyists may take on more than they can handle and therefore, do not receive the proper satisfaction. ▸

After hatching, the hen will feed and brood her young continuously. By the time the young are 10 or 12 days old they are covered with pin feathers. Feeding by both parents continues through the growth process and good parents will always have the crops of their young full. The young will soon begin playing with seed and experiment in cracking and shelling. The parents then cut down on feeding the young a little at a time until they are eating enough to survive on their own.

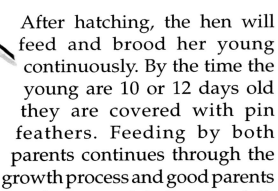

Newly independent, these two young Green Canaries have just been weaned. It is still difficult to determine the sex of the young canaries. ▸

WEANING THE YOUNG

Cultivation of the crest is one of the principle features of the Gloster Fancy. Whether nestlings are Coronas or Consorts becomes apparent as they feather in. ▸

By this time the mother canary is setting the nest and is ready to lay another clutch of eggs and raise her second set of offspring. This rapid growth process is amazing to watch. At times it seems as though the young birds are growing right before your eyes. The young consume a tremendous amount of food to accomodate their growth. Plenty of fresh food must be provided for the birds at this time.

▸ Young canaries are weaned at 21 days but still look to their mother for advise. They are not consuming enough food on their own to sustain their current weight nor add to it for the rapid growth they are experiencing. They are, however, playing with seeds and learning how to crack them open. Chicks become lazy and will not want to become weaned which places a great burden on the mother bird.

At 16 days old the chicks are balls of fluff, and by 21 days they are completely feathered. By this time they have short tails with a little down remaining on their head and are ready to leave the nest. This chick is nearly full fledged but still in the nest.

▸ A hatchling of only a day or two begs for food. It will seem as if young canaries are always being fed, but considering their rapid growth rate, it is natural.

IDENTIFICATION BANDS

At seven to ten days old, the young are old enough to be banded. Identification bands are used by breeders to record and track important information such as, the color of the parents, the year born, how many young were raised by a given pair in a year, etc. Banding young birds is also beneficial to breeders who sell their stock off. A breeder can easily supply the consumer with the genetic history of the bird being sold from the information recorded from the band number.

▶ To place a band on the leg of a young canary, take the foot to be banded between your fingers in such a manner that the back toe points toward the back and the other toes are stretched toward the front.

◆ Identification bands help to keep track of important information such as a bird's age.

▶ Now place the ring over the toes toward the front, pass over the back as well, and continue a little further up the leg.

◆ Bands are available in different colors with numbers, years, and even breeders initials ingraved for better records.

The ring should now be properly in place around the leg. ▶

Only banded birds may enter exhibitions. Rings can be ordered through canary associations and clubs that are affiliated with such exhibitions. ◆

IDENTIFICATION BANDS

In breeding as a hobby only, bands are not necessary, but can be helpful when breeding for specific colors or variations.

Some hens try to remove the bands from the nest as if they were foreign particles and as a result, toss one of the babies out.

A breeder will be able to recognize his bands or colleague's bands when purchasing future stock because each band is unique. The band is placed on the birds leg by pushing it over the front toes. When these emerge, they are held between the index finger of one hand, while the thumb and index finger of the hand holding the bird are used to pull the band onto the leg and over the hind toe. After banding one should keep an eye on the mother to see how she reacts to the bands.

If you sell your young birds to a pet shop, the only way a dealer will know your birds at a later date is by the identification bands.

Occasionally, a canary can injure its leg by the band becoming caught up on the cage. If you are not using the bird for show, you may wish to cut the band off and mark the bird in some other manner that can not cause harm.

GENETICS

A full understanding of genetics is not necessary but basics will help produce the desired results. All animals inherit traits from each parent through genes. Genes act as tiny units of information which tell the body cells how to develop. Genes are held together by chromosomes. Chromosomes are always in identical pairs except in sex cells. If in the inheritance of a color, the genes coming from the male and the female are the same, the young bird will resemble its parents and be homozygous, or pure, for this color.

◆ Experienced bird keepers wishing to breed for specific color, shape, and song must be informed somewhat of genetics so that the desired offspring are produced.

◆ Genes determine hereditary characteristics such as the color of a bird. In the past, the successful production of birds and color varieties relied more or less on chance, but now the knowledge of the principles of inheritence are used to preserve mutations and produce new colors.

◆ A young canary receives half of its chromosomes from its father, and half from its mother. Genes, the factors of all the different hereditary traits, are located on the chromosomes. Chromosomes and their genes are present in pairs in every cell nucleus.

GENETICS

Dominant and recessive factors are extremely important to the heredity of Canaries. This is how the many different breeds and color varieties arose. In the wild, mutations usually disappear very quickly since the traits of normal breeds dominate.

If the parents differ in color and the differing genes are not effective, the young receiving the appropriate gene from each parent, will show the color of the genetically more effective parent. This is an example of dominant/recessive inheritance. Such young are heterozygous or impure for its color.

With the knowledge that is now available on the principles of inheritance, we are able to preserve mutations and create new colors of canaries through specific breeding stock selections.

Through cross-breeding with the Red Hooded Siskin, the Red-Factor Canary was produced. Cross-breeding assured that the red was incorporated in the breed's hereditary material.

Certain gene combinations can be lethal to the sex cells, zygote, embryo, or to the newly hatched chick. The crest mutation being one of them.

BIRD SHOWS

Some breeders bathe their birds prior to each show. This should be done about two days before the show so that the bird's natural oils can give the feathers a final sparkle. ▶

▲ A typical compact show exhibition cage. A canary breeder has two moments in his life that are regarded as highly memorable: the first family of canaries that he raised, and the first show that he won.

Of the many different varieties of canaries, there are equally, if not more, varieties of show competitions. Each variety has its own standard show cage and way of being prepared for the show. They are judged on a variety of specifications and awards are made. The show birds are trained while very young. The object of training is to duplicate the conditions under which the bird will be exhibited. The more familiar the bird is to unusual sight and sound, the better. After this, it is trained to assume a position or to sing on command.

A few examples of the colorful rewards of the bird show. This creates excitement for the hobbyist. Once you are a champion at a show, you remain that forever. Even if you drop out of the hobby and return after a few years. ▶

BIRD SHOWS

◀ During a show, it is important that food and water be available for the bird. During judging, however, one should check with the association's regulations in regards to food and water in the cage.

The exhibition season runs from September through April. The biggest shows are held from October to February. Unlike most livestock shows where the animal gets the status, it is the breeder who gains the status when showing birds. Therefore for many keepers, exhibiting is one of the most exciting aspects of the hobby.

◀ Different canary varieties have their own special show cage designs. Be sure your cages are spotless. Should your bird be equal to another, the general presentation of the exhibit and its cage may be the deciding factor.

◀ Do not attempt to show too many birds in one season. This quickly becomes frustrating when some are not up to par when the show date arrives.

MOLTING

These two canaries are almost finished their molt and have not been color-fed steadily. Their color will remain this way until their next molt. Color feeding agents must be fed prior to the molt. ▶

It is advisable to supply color food all year 'round. Additional foods that contain carotene, such as carrots, are also advisable to feed as natural color enhancers.

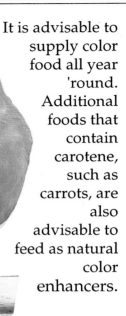

It is normal and natural for a bird to molt. At eight to ten weeks old, canaries begin their first molt. This involves a replacement of their lesser colored feathers with adult plumage color that is retained until the next year during the next molt. Molting drains the bird of energy. It is imperative that the bird not be handled or bred during the molting process because the added stress could prove detrimental to its health.

◄ Regular bathing facilities should be provided for the bird during the molt to ease the bird when preening.

Birds typically molt during the hot weather. The entire process should be complete in 3-5 months. ▶

MOLTING

The key to a quick molt is to leave the bird alone as much as possible, in a cool, but not drafty area, and to feed it a highly nutritious and varied diet.

Fresh air, sunshine and rain, all have a positive effect on molting and plumage by helping the feathers grow in at a quicker pace and in a better condition than in the absence of it. Canaries usually molt beginning on the breast and gradually extending to the whole body, ending with the feathers on the head.

A molt makes tremendous demands on the bird's metabolism and therefore a highly nutritious and varied diet is required during this time.

Remember that colorfed varieties should be receiving their coloring agent before the onset of the molt. Any bird will turn red if artificial coloring agents are supplied in its diet. A true Red-factor is one that can use natural carotene to enhance its coloring.

DISEASES

Sweating sickness is when the lower part of the hen's body is wet, sticky, and rather dirty. A new nest is required. ▶

Asthma affects the breathing of the bird and can be caused by dust in unclean seed. This can be remedied by using a tiny amount of Vicks in the nostrils of the bird. ▶

There are many ways in which diseases can be transmitted and therefore guarding against them is impossible. There are, however, certain precautions that may be taken to try to prevent illness. Diarrhea is most common in a bird when its diet is changed. Too much of a food that the bird is not in the habit of eating will cause loose droppings. Foods that will bind the bird, pound cake or hard boiled egg, will remedy this. Inflammation of the eye frequently occurs if the bird has been in a draft, or kept in a room where a lot of heavy smoking goes on. Obtain an antibiotic ointment that requires a prescription from a veterinarian.

A disease may affect a number of birds if not acted upon in the early stages. It is important to remove an ill bird as soon as it shows any signs that it may be sick. Illness spreads quickly in birds and if not recognized in the early stages can reach epidemic levels. ▸

In canary keeping, preventative health maintenance is easier to achieve than the cure of any disease. ▸

A bird's posture can give clear indication as to its state of health. ➤

A clean kept, well-fed bird has little risk of becomming ill. Unfortunately, this is not a sure way to guard against illness. The best safeguard is to know your bird and its habits well and the slightest change in them will tip you off to an illness.

Scaly feet is caused by a tiny scale mite which gets under the scales of the birds feet. The feet develop hard scales and become red and inflamed. If this should occur, consult a reliable pet shop dealer or a veterinarian and request a medication that will help. ▸

INDEX

Page numbers in **boldface** refer to illustrations.